What Is Phonemic Awareness?

Phonemic awareness is knowing how spoken language works. Young students need to have a strong understanding of spoken language before they can understand written language. Phonemically aware students know that sounds are the building blocks of our language. They can:

- hear the sounds that make up words.
- see relationships between sounds
- change or rearrange sounds to create new words.

Phonemic awareness is taught through oral games and activities presented sequentially. A student begins with an awareness of spoken words, then becomes aware of syllables, onsets, and rimes (see definitions, below), and finally, individual sounds within a word.

Phonemic awareness is not phonics, but the two are dependent upon each other. Phonemic awareness focuses on the sound units (phonemes) that form spoken words. Phonics associates sounds with written symbols. Together the two help students develop word recognition skills. Phonemic awareness comes before phonics. Young students must be able to hear and manipulate oral sound patterns before they relate them to print.

As you begin to work with letter-sound associations, continue to practice and reinforce phonemic awareness. The lessons in weeks 30-34 use the rhyme of the week to both reinforce phonemic awareness and provide practice in letter-sound associations.

The Vocabulary of Phonemic Awareness

phoneme - an individual sound; /t/ is a phoneme, so is /ow/.

onset - beginning sound(s); sounds before the first vowel. In bat, b is the onset; in stop, st is the onset.

rime - the first vowel and the rest of the word; the rime in man is an; the rime in stand is and.

How to Use This Book

Assessing Phonemic Awareness
A Phonemic Awareness Inventory is provided on Page 112 and the inside back cover. Give the inventory orally to individual students. Knowing your students' current awareness level will help you to know where to begin and what to emphasize in your instruction. Use the inventory periodically throughout the year to assess student progress.

How the Lessons Are Presented
The language play lessons in this book are divided into 34 weekly sections following this format:

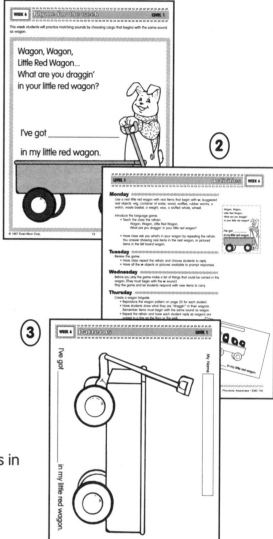

① **Rhyme for the Week** - a poem, chant, or language game to be used throughout the week.

② **Activities** - a five- to ten-minute activity for each day, Monday through Friday, using the poem, chant, or game.

③ **Patterns** - reproducible patterns to use in the week's lessons.

The lessons increase in difficulty, moving through the five levels of phonemic awareness. The most difficult lessons involve letter recognition and assume that students have mastered basic letter/sound relationships.

Patterns to Use
Use the patterns provided in this book to facilitate your lessons in a number of ways:
- Make characters for felt board presentations.
- Add magnetic tape and use on your chalk board.
- Create puppets.
- Make overhead transparencies.
- Make flash cards.

Reproduce and laminate the alphabet cards on pages 105-111 and use them as a part of your daily routine.

Work with this simple good morning rhyme to emphasize the rhythm of the words and the idea of response. Patterns for making puppets to demonstrate response are found on page 5.

Good morning. Good morning.
And how do you do?

Good morning. Good morning.
I'm fine. How 'bout you?

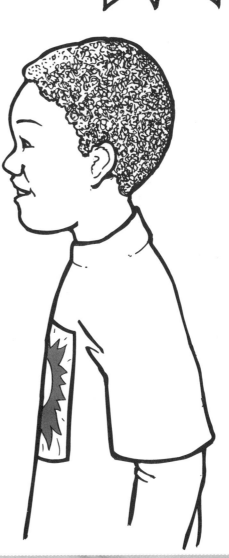

Monday

Use two puppets (see patterns on page 5) to model the rhyme. One puppet "says" the first two lines; the second puppet responds by saying the last two lines.

Say the first two lines again and have students echo you, using their pointer fingers as puppets. Repeat with the second set of lines.

Say the entire rhyme several times.

The Echo Technique

The directions for teaching most of the rhymes in this book will suggest that the students echo parts of the rhyme. This simply means that students repeat back what you have just said. The amount you ask students to echo will depend on the average auditory memory of the group. Start with one line or maybe even part of a line. With consistent practice, students will be able to remember and echo larger sections of the rhymes.

Tuesday

Review the rhyme as whole group question/answer:
• You say the first two lines.
• The class answers with the last two lines.

Then reverse, letting the class question and you answer.

Wednesday

Let pairs of students act out the rhyme as the class recites.

Thursday

Divide into pairs. One person from each pair will do the first two lines, and the other person will do the second two lines.

Begin with a practice where all "first-line" students recite together; then all the "second-line" students recite together.

Friday

Pairs recite and act out the rhyme without class support.

fold

fold

Students follow directions and, at the same time, listen to the way that words change when sounds are manipulated.

Ship, shop, shup,
Let's stand up.

Clin, clan, clown,
Now sit down.

Monday

Recite the rhyme:
- Have students follow the directions to stand and sit.
- Invite students to say the rhyme with you.

Tuesday

Review the rhyme with students acting out the directions as you recite:
- Say the first line softly and then say the second line loudly.
- Do the same for third and fourth lines.
- Reverse the soft and loud parts as you say the rhyme again.

Wednesday

Review the rhyme. You repeat the cue line (ship, shop, shup or clin, clan, clown) and have students as a group repeat the next line, standing or sitting appropriately.

Thursday

Have groups of students direct the class by reciting the rhyme. You and the rest of the class follow the directions.

Friday

Let individual students direct the class in standing and sitting by reciting the rhyme.

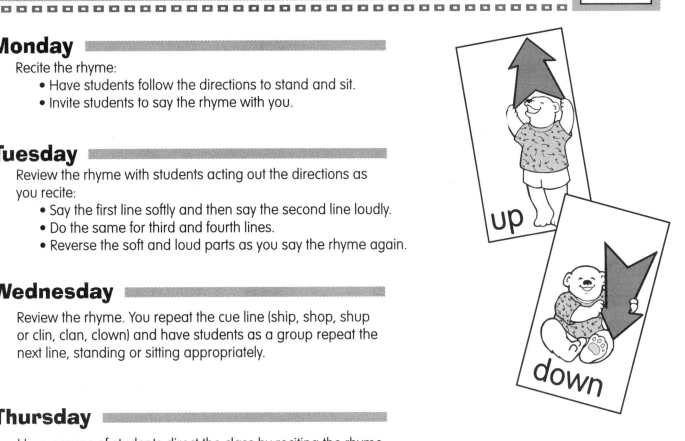

As your students become familiar with the rhyme, designate one student as the Up person and one student as the Down person. Give them rulers with signs below attached and have them signal the words *up* and *down* at the appropriate times.

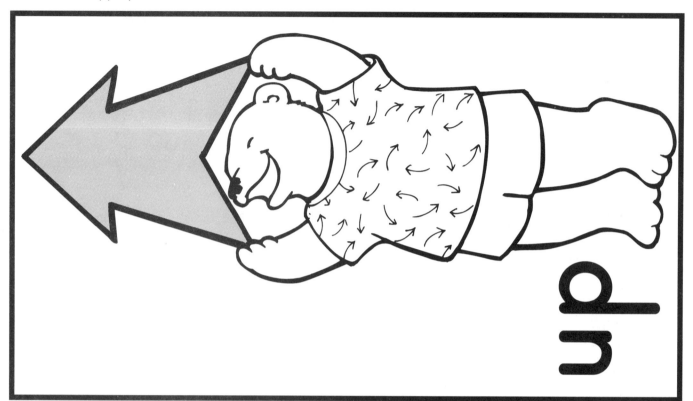

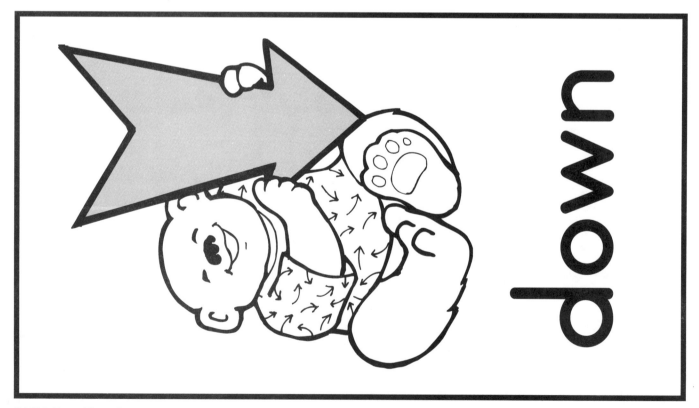

Go slowly at first as you learn this counting rhyme. Then speed up as your class gains proficiency in counting backwards.

1...2...3
Look at me.

4...5...6
See my tricks.

7...8...9
I feel fine.

9...8...7...

6...5...4...

3...2...1

Now I'm done!

Phonemic Awareness • EMC 740

Monday

Introduce the counting rhyme to students:
- Say the rhyme through once.
- Say the rhyme again, letting students echo the three pairs of lines.
- Invite students to say the rhyme with you.

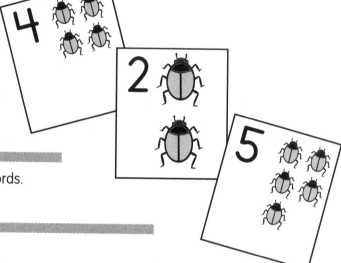

1...2...3
Look at me.

4...5...6
See my tricks.

7...8...9
I feel fine.

9...8...7...
6...5...4...
3...2...1

Now I'm done!

Tuesday

Count and clap the rhyme. Clap once on each number several times. Remember to go slowly at first.

Wednesday

Use the number cards on page 11. Say the rhyme and hold up a card each time a number is named.

Hand out number cards and have students hold them up at the appropriate times.

Thursday

Recite the rhyme. Have students identify rhyming words.

Friday

Choose one child to be a performer.
- Class chants 1...2...3
- Performer says "Look at me!" and jumps up.
- Class chants 4...5...6
- Performer says "See my tricks!" and twirls or jumps or somersaults....
- Class chants 7...8...9
- Performer bows and says "I feel fine."
- Class chants 9...8...7...6...5...4...3...2...1
- Performer returns to place and sits down, saying, "Now I'm done."

1	2	3
4	5	6
7	8	9

Develop vocabulary and begin to recognize sound patterns.

Tick Tock Tipper
Where is your zipper?

Tick Tock Tutton
Where is your button?

Tick Tock Tocket
Where is your pocket?

Tick Tock Teeve
Where is your sleeve?

Tick Tock Too
Where is your shoe?

Tick Tock Tollar
Where is your collar?

Monday

Introduce the rhyme:
- As you recite, have students show you their zippers, buttons, pockets, sleeves, shoes, and collars when you ask where they are.
- For each couplet, repeat each line and have students echo you.
- Then repeat the couplet and have students echo both lines.

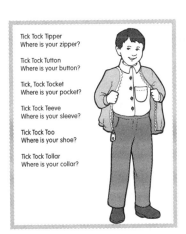

Tick Tock Tipper
Where is your zipper?

Tick Tock Tutton
Where is your button?

Tick, Tock Tocket
Where is your pocket?

Tick Tock Teeve
Where is your sleeve?

Tick Tock Too
Where is your shoe?

Tick Tock Tollar
Where is your collar?

Tuesday

Review the rhyme:
- You say the first line of each couplet and invite students to give the second line.
- Invite students to chant the entire rhyme with you.
- Choose one student to be the pointer and point to a student after each question. That student will show the clothing part named.

Wednesday

Reproduce a set of the picture cards on page 14 for each student.

As you say the rhyme, leave out the word that names the clothing part. Students hold up the picture card for the word that would complete that part of the rhyme.

Divide the class into two groups. One group chants the rhyme, leaving out the name of the clothing part; the other group says the missing word and shows the picture. Switch roles and repeat.

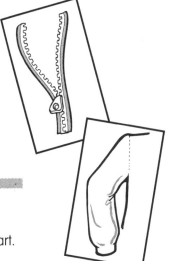

Thursday

Review the rhyme:
- Point out that the rhyme has four parts. Recite each part.
- Ask students to listen closely and tell you what is the same about each part. (Each part says Tick Tock _____ and Where is your _____)
- Then ask students to tell what is different about each part. (Each part asks where something different is and each part has a different word after Tick Tock.)
- Talk briefly about the relationship between the different words and the different items of clothing. (Point out that the different word after Tick Tock always has a /t/ at the beginning and rhymes with the clothing item.

Friday

After reviewing the rhyme, make up new verses for new items of clothing.

Tick Tock Toot
Where is your boot?

Tick Tock Toat
Where is your coat?

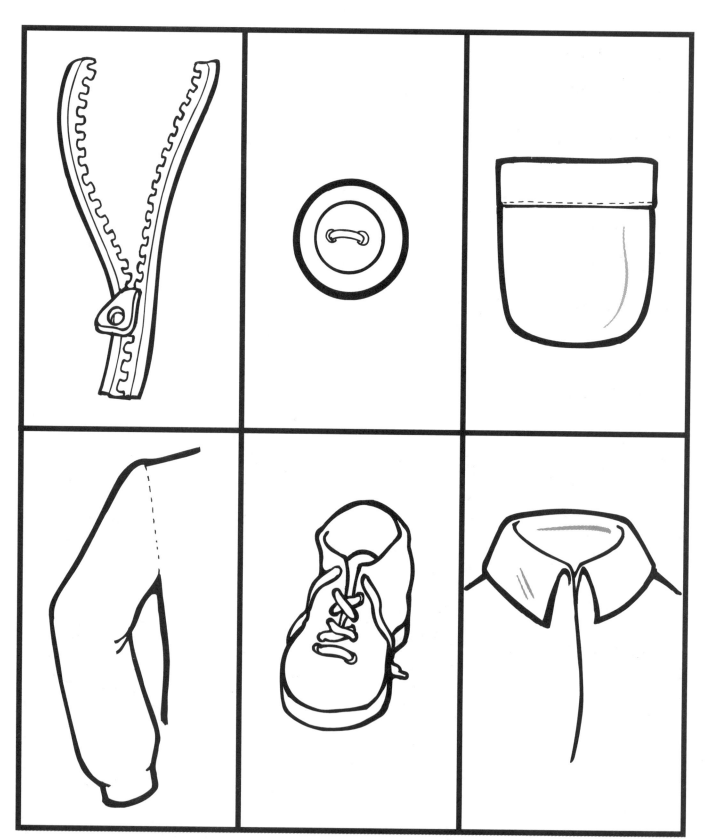

Learn this chant by echoing, then say it often at the end of each day.

I'm done.
I'm done.
I've got to run.

So long.
So long.
A farewell song.

Good-bye.
Good-bye.
But please don't cry.

Adieu.
Adieu.
From me to you.

I'm done.
I'm done.
I've got to run.

So long.
So long.
A farewell song.

Good-bye.
Good-bye.
But please don't cry.

Adieu.
Adieu.
From me to you.

Monday

Introduce the chant:
- Recite the chant once.
- Repeat the chant, having the class echo the lines as you say them. Do two or three lines at once, depending on the abilities of your students.

Tuesday

Review the chant:
- Have students echo each part of the chant.
- Have students identify the rhyming words in each verse.
  (done—run   long—song   bye—cry   adieu—you)

Wednesday

Review the chant:
- Divide the class into two lines, facing each other.
- Have one line say the first verse.
  The other line replies with the second verse.
  First line says the third verse. Second line says the fourth verse.
- Both lines wave to each other, turn, and "leave."

Thursday

Wave to the beat as you recite the chant. (Wave good-bye on every syllable.)

March and wave at the same time.

Count to find out how many beats are in each verse. (Each syllable = one beat, so every stanza has 8 beats.)

Friday

Reproduce the form on page 17. Have each student draw themselves waving good-bye.

Post the pictures around the doorway or make a class book.

Recite the chant together as you leave for the day.

Good-Bye

My Name

Good-Bye

 Phonemic Awareness • EMC 740

This week students will practice matching sounds by choosing cargo that begins with the same sound as wagon.

Wagon, Wagon,
Little Red Wagon...
What are you draggin'
in your little red wagon?

I've got _____
in my little red wagon.

Monday

Use a real little red wagon with real items that begin with **w**; (some suggested real objects: wig, container of water, wood, waffles, rubber worms, a watch, waste basket, a weight, wax, a stuffed whale, wheel)

Introduce the language game:
- Teach the class the refrain:
  Wagon, Wagon, Little Red Wagon,
  What are you draggin' in your little red wagon?

- Have class ask you what's in the wagon by repeating the refrain. You answer showing real items in the real wagon, or pictured items in the felt board wagon.

Wagon, Wagon,
Little Red Wagon...
What are you draggin'
in your little red wagon?

I've got _____
in my little red wagon.

Tuesday

Review the game:
- Have class repeat the refrain and choose students to reply.
- Have all the **w** objects or pictures available to prompt responses.

Wednesday

Before you play the game make a list of things that could be carried in the wagon. (They must begin with the **w** sound.)
Play the game and let students respond with new items to carry.

Thursday

Create a wagon brigade:
- Reproduce the wagon pattern on page 20 for each student.
- Have students draw what they are "draggin'" in their wagons. Remember items must begin with the same sound as wagon.
- Repeat the refrain and have each student reply as wagons are posted in a line on the floor or the wall.

Friday

Celebrate your wagon brigade by reading it.
Personalize the refrain for your class.

Wagon, Wagon, Little Red Wagon,
What is Jose draggin' in his little red wagon?

Jose has worms in his little red wagon.

Wagon, Wagon, Little Red Wagon,
What is Penny draggin' in her little red wagon?

Penny has water in her little red wagon.

My Name

I've got **wheels** in my little red wagon.

My Name

I've got _____ in my little red wagon.

Sing this rhyme to the tune of "Where Is Thumbkin?"

Where's the sunshine?
Where's the sunshine?

Here it is.
Here it is.

Come and shine on our class.
Yes, I'll shine on your class.

What a day!
What a day!

Monday

Teach the song having students echo each part.
Use sun puppet (page 23) to help students understand when
the sun is talking.

Where's the sunshine?	
Where's the sunshine?	*(left hand holding puppet behind back)*
Here it is.	
Here it is.	*(left hand with puppet moves forward)*
Come and shine on our class.	*(singing to puppet)*
Yes, I'll shine on your class.	*(puppet responds)*
What a day!	
What a day!	*(left hand and sun go back behind back)*

Tuesday

Reproduce the sun puppet for students to use as they sing the song.
Review and sing song several times.

Wednesday

Review the song. Have students clap the rhythm as they sing.
(one clap per syllable)

Thursday

Review clapping:
- Sing a line. Clap the same line without singing.
- Sing the next line. Clap the next line, etc.

Friday

Have half of the class sing and clap one line while the other
half of the class counts the number of syllabic beats.

Record the numbers and talk about the pattern.

Count hats and syllables with this rhyme.

One hat,
    two hats
        three hats
            four

Now please help me
count some more.

Monday

Use real hats or hat patterns on page 26 as you introduce the couplet.
- Arrange the hats in a pyramid - a row of four hats as the base, then three hats, then two hats, and one hat on top.
- Point to the rows as you repeat the words.

Repeat several times, letting children join in the counting.

Tuesday

Review the couplet by playing a counting game:
- Say the couplet.
- After the second line, give one student a number of hats made from the patterns on page 26. Depending on the counting abilities of your students, you may need to reproduce several pages of hats.
- The student counts the hats out loud.
- Give the hats to several other students to count.

Wednesday

Clap as you recite the couplet to the students.

Have the students recite and clap with you.

Have half of the class clap the beat while the others count the number of syllables in each line.

One hat,
two hats,
three hats,
four

Now please help me count some more.

Thursday

Substitute another word for hat. (shoe, chair, block, finger, etc.) Say the couplet and have the students repeat it.

Clap and count to determine if the change changed the number of syllables.

Friday

Have each student illustrate a version of the couplet:
- Give students a sheet of white paper.
- Students draw a pyramid of their things, starting with a base of four as with the hats.
- Students label each row of the pyramid with a number.

Have students count the number of syllables in each line of their couplets.

Practice the days of the week and match sounds at the same time.

It's Monday.

It's Monday.

Let's have a fun day!

It's Tuesday.

It's Tuesday.

Shine-up-your-shoes day.

It's Wednesday.

It's Wednesday.

Visit-with-your-friends day.

It's Thursday.

It's Thursday.

When-the-cat-purrs day.

It's Friday.

It's Friday.

Look-up-in-the-sky day.

Monday

Reference your classroom calendar as you introduce the poem. Read the poem several times. Invite students to recite with you.

Let students say the first two lines of each stanza; you say the third. If students are ready, reverse roles and recite the poem again.

It's Monday.
It's Monday.
Let's have a fun day!

It's Tuesday.
It's Tuesday.
Shine-up-your-shoes day.

It's Wednesday.
It's Wednesday.
Visit-with-your-friends day.

It's Thursday.
It's Thursday.
When-the-cat-purrs day.

It's Friday.
It's Friday.
Look-up-in-the-sky day.

Tuesday

Teacher recites the poem once; students join in the second time through. Ask students to identify the rhyming words.

Monday	fun day
Tuesday	shoes day
Wednesday	friends day
Thursday	purrs day
Friday	sky day

Wednesday

Reproduce the word cards on page 29. (Each student will need one word card for Thursday's activity.) As the class says the poem, teacher holds up the correct word card each time the word is said.

After you have demonstrated, let students take turns holding up the cards at the appropriate times.

Monday
Wednesday
Friday

Thursday

Give each student a word card. Station a student with each "day" in five different spots. Each shows their card and quietly chants the word.

As the poem is recited, students quietly move to the appropriate spot to match the word card they hold.

Friday

Review the poem:
Recite it together several times.
Ask the students to tell which day is...
   a shoes day
   a purrs day
   a fun day
   a sky day
   a friends day

 Monday

 Tuesday

 Wednesday

 Thursday

 Friday

Use the clock-face picture cards on page 101 as you recite this verse and practice sound matching.

Early in the morning
when the clock says four
I'll get up and open my door.

Early in the morning
when the clock says five
I'll start the car and go for a drive.

Early in the morning
when the clock says six
I'll take time to feed the chicks.

Early in the morning
when the clock says seven
I'll pull up the blanket and sleep 'til eleven.

Early in the morning
when the clock says four
I'll get up and open my door.　**4:00**

Early in the morning
when the clock says five
I'll start the car and go for a drive.　**5:00**

Early in the morning
when the clock says six
I'll take time to feed the chicks.　**6:00**

Early in the morning
when the clock says seven
I'll pull up the blanket and sleep 'til eleven.　**7:00**

Monday

Reproduce the clock faces on page 32. Say the poem to the class, holding up the correct clock for each verse.

Recite the poem again and have students act out each verse.

Tuesday

Review the poem:
- Have the students say the first line of each couplet (hold up the clock faces to cue the correct time). You say the second lines.
- Ask students to identify the rhyming words. Hold up a clock face and say, "The clock says (four)." Students respond with the rhyming word, "door."

Wednesday

Review the poem:
- Pass out the clock faces and the picture cards for door, drive, chicks, eleven.
- Students with cards need to form rhyming pairs.
    (four—door　five—drive　six—chicks　seven—eleven)
- Have student pairs lead the class in reciting their stanza of the poem.

Thursday

As a class write another verse for the poem:
- Start with "Early in the morning when the clock says eight."
- Think of things that rhyme with the word eight.
    gate　late　fate　wait　straight
- Choose one thing and put it into a sentence that tells something you could do.
    I heard someone open the gate.
    Mother called, "Get up, you're late!"
- Record your new verse and read it together.

Friday

Have students draw what they do at a specific hour. (A rhyme is not necessary.) Write on each drawing. For example:
    At _____, I _____ .
    (At four, I snore.)

Have students share their pictures.

Students will separate the words in this chant into individual phonemes.

Mix it fast.
Mix Mix Mix

Mix it slow.
/m/ /i/ /ks/ /m/ /i/ /ks/ /m/ /i/ /ks/

Mix it high.
Mix Mix Mix

Mix it low.
Mix Mix Mix

Monday

Introduce the chant:
- Use a mixing bowl and spoon. Stir the speed of the words.
- After the line, "Mix it slow," separate mix into sounds (phonemes) — /m/ /i/ /ks/.
- After the line, "Mix it high," say the words in a high voice.
- After the line, "Mix it low," say the words in a deep voice.

Have students echo each line after you.

Tuesday

Reproduce the direction cards on page 35. Review the chant by having students echo each line.

Have students say the second line as you hold up each direction card:
- Teacher: Mix it fast.
- Students: Mix Mix Mix
- Teacher: Mix it slow.
- Students: /m/ /i/ /ks/ /m/ /i/ /ks/ /m/ /i/ /ks/

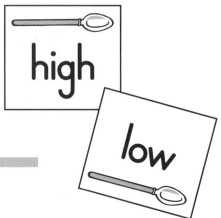

Wednesday

Say the chant together. Discuss its pattern. (fast, slow, high, low)
Substitute several different words for mix.

Sing it. (/s/ /i/ /ng/)
Kick it. (/k/ /i/ /k/)
Wave it. (/w/ /a/ /v/)

Thursday

Substitute different words again.

Snap it. (/s/ /n/ /a/ /p/)
Stamp it. (/s/ /t/ /a/ /m/ /p/)
Shake it. (/sh/ /a/ /k/)

Friday

Have individual students lead the chant, choosing an action verb of their choice.

Question & answer response games are a great way to practice syllable counting.

Doodle doodle doodle do
Can you jump? I'll watch you.

Doodle doodle doodle dee
I can jump. Look at me.

Monday

Introduce the chant:
- Use any two puppets you have to demonstrate the question and answer.
- Have students echo you as you say the poem again one line at a time. Repeat, doing two lines at a time.
- Invite two students to use the puppets as the class chants the entire rhyme.

Doodle doodle doodle do
Can you jump? I'll watch you.

Doodle doodle doodle dee
I can jump. Look at me.

Tuesday

Review the chant:
- Have students echo each part of the rhyme.
- Tap the beat as you say the poem again.
- Then have half the class tap the beat while the others count the number of syllables.

Wednesday

Change the chant by substituting a different action.

dance
bow
hop
salute

Count the syllables in each chant. Have students tell which actions change the syllable count. Divide the action words into syllables.

Thursday

Choose students to lead the chant:
- Each student leader chooses an action.
- The student chants
    "Doodle doodle doodle do
    Can you _____? I'll watch you."
- The class responds with the second part of the chant and demonstrates the action.

Friday

Create a class book:
- Reproduce page 38 for individual students.
- Students draw themselves doing something.
- Teacher fills in the action word.
- Have students chant their pages.

Doodle doodle doodle dee
I can jump Look at me!

My Name

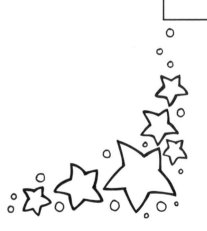

Doodle doodle doodle dee

I can

_____. Look at me!

Enjoy the nonsense refrain for this rhyme, as you practice matching sounds.

There was a little bug.

It lived inside a rug.

It loved to hop.

hop hoppy hop

hop hoppy hop

hop hoppy

hop hoppy

hop hoppy hop

Monday

Introduce the couplet with the pop-up little bug (pattern on page 41).
As you chant the refrain, make the bug "hop" in time with the beat of the words -- hop (bug hops once), hoppy (bug hops twice quickly).
Have students repeat the couplet and refrain with you several times.

There was a little bug.
It lived inside a rug.
It loved to hop.

hop hoppy hop
hop hoppy hop
hop hoppy
hop hoppy
hop hoppy hop

Tuesday

Review couplet and refrain. Echo as necessary until students are comfortable with the rhyme.

Then have students repeat the couplet and hop to the beat of the refrain.

Wednesday

Substitute several different actions:
  crawl, roll, run, jump

Practice the refrains following the pattern used for hop in the rhyme:
For example:
  jump jumpy jump
  jump jumpy jump
  jump jumpy
  jump jumpy
  jump jumpy jump

Thursday

Have students choose actions for the bugs. Challenge them to create their own refrains following the pattern.

Friday

Finish the week with more student choice actions. If students need a challenge, suggest that the bug might do two things.

There was a little bug.
It lived on a rug.
It loved to eat and play.

    eat eaty eat and play playie play
    eat eaty eat and play playie play
    eat eaty, play playie
    eat eaty, play playie
    eat eaty eat, and play playie play

Glue the bug to a craft stick. Cut the slit in the rug with an Exacto® knife.

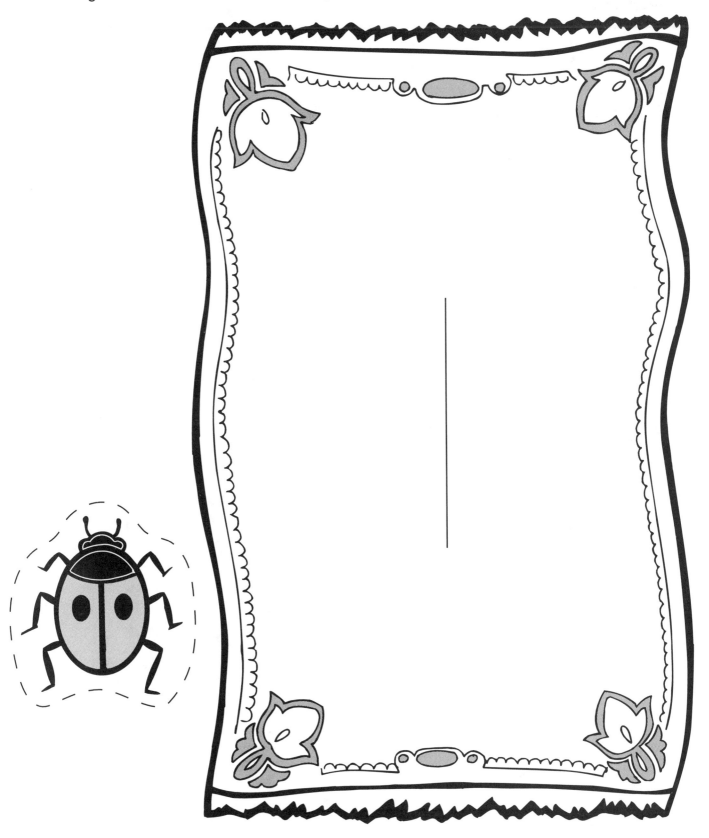

Use these two poems to practice splitting words into syllables.

Bird, Bird
Can you fly?
Flap your
wings
Up to the sky.

Puppy, Puppy
Can you run?
Come outside.
Have some fun.

Monday

Recite the bird poem and have class echo you, one or two lines at a time. Students might flap their wings to the syllable beat.

Bird, Bird
Can you fly?
Flap your wings
Up to the sky.

Tuesday

Recite the bird poem with class.

Show picture cards (patterns on page 44) of things that might be in the sky. Have students name each thing.

Model how to flap each word into syllables:
- Hold up your hands, palms toward you; move your hands toward each other until the thumbs cross, forming a "bird."
- Flap one wing on the first syllable and the other wing on the second syllable.

Students should practice flapping each of the words.

Wednesday

Recite the bird poem together. Have students name things that they might see in the sky.

"Flap" each of the suggestions to the syllable beat. Count the flaps.

Thursday

Introduce the puppy poem, having students learn it by echoing. Have students repeat the poem, moving their feet up and down in place on the syllable beat.

Friday

After reciting the puppy poem, have students suggest other things that a puppy might do.

Move feet up and down in place to each of the words to split it into syllables.

Puppy, Puppy
Can you run?
Come outside.
Have some fun.

Chant this riddle as you help students blend sounds together and match letters to sounds.

Start with _____

End with _____

Put it together

And you have _____

Monday

Chant the riddle, filling the blanks with an onset and rime that blend into one of your students' names. Have the class supply the name.
For example:

> Start with /j/.
> End with /ill/.
> Put it together
> And you have Jill.

Repeat with several names.

Tuesday

Chant the riddle using each student's name.

Wednesday

Reproduce the puzzle pattern on page 47.

Help each student to write the beginning letter of his/her name on the smaller puzzle section and the rest of the name on the larger section.

Cut the puzzle apart on the line.

Each student can chant their own name riddle.

Start with /m/.	Hold up piece with M on it.
End with /ark/.	Hold up piece with ark on it.
Put it together	
And you have Mark.	Move the pieces together to form Mark.

Thursday

Use the chant to name simple words from current classroom literature.
For example:

> Start with /w/.
> End with /aldo/.
> Put it together
> And you have Waldo.

Friday

Make puzzle pieces for several different words using the pattern on page 47.
Pass one puzzle piece to each student.

You lead the chant. As you say an onset or a rime, the students holding those puzzle pieces stand. They move to the front of the room as the class chants, "Put it together." Then the whole class says, "And you have _____."

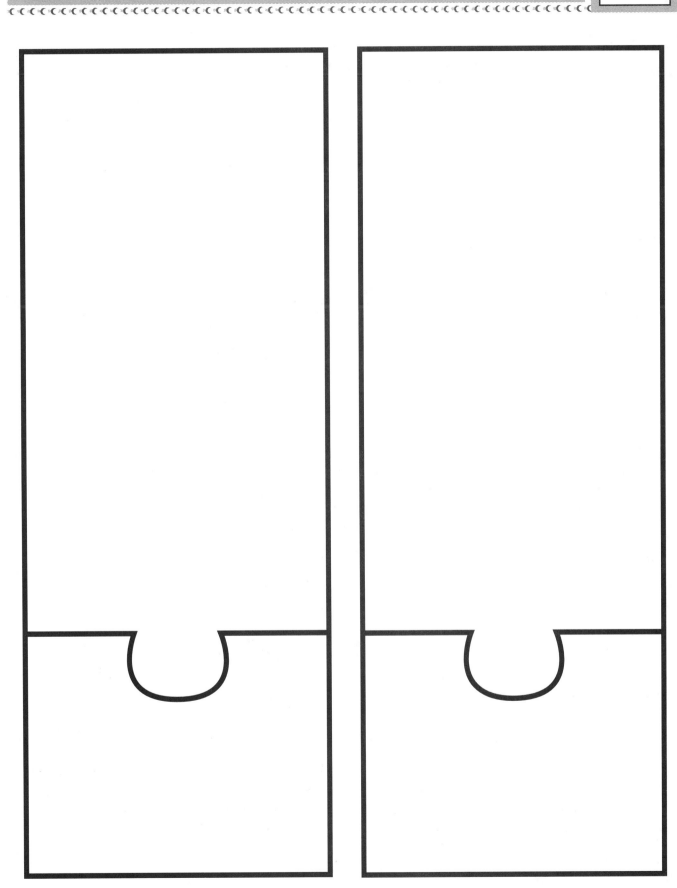

Developing vocabulary and identifying onset-rime go hand in hand.

What shall I call...

A grown-up calf?   a cow

A grown-up pup?   a dog

A grown-up boy?   a man

A grown-up kitten?   a cat

A grown-up colt?   a horse

A grown-up kid?   a goat

Monday

Use the picture cards on page 50 to introduce the baby and adult animal terminology:
- Show a baby animal picture. (picture of a puppy)
- Ask students to identify the name for the baby animal. (pup)
- Show the adult animal picture. (picture of a dog)
- Ask students to identify the name for the adult animal. (dog)

Read the chant questions and answers as you show the matching pictures. Read the questions again and have students supply the answers.

Tuesday

Recite the chant as you review baby/adult animal names. Have students identify onsets and rimes in each name. For example:

> boy—the onset is /b/; the rime is /oy/.

Create new words (including nonsense words) by substituting different onsets – roy, coy, moy, toy...

Wednesday

Review the baby/adult names by playing a question/answer game:
- Ask "What shall I call a grown-up colt?"
- Point to a student for the answer. "A horse."
- The student next to the first student must create a new word by substituting a different onset. "A dorse."
- The next student does the same. "A morse."
- Take one more new word from another student. "A borse."
- And the class replies. "A horse."

Thursday

Before the lesson, write the onsets and rimes for the animal names on sentence strip cards. Display the onset and rime cards in a pocket chart. Show a picture of an animal. Have students choose the onset and rime to form the name of the animal.

Friday

Students draw to create their own baby/adult pair.
- Students draw a baby and adult animal.
- Students show picture to class and say "What shall I call a grown-up _____? A _____". (girl/woman)

Record the new questions and answers to make a new class chant.

Practice sound matching and phoneme blending with the -og family.

Five little froggies sitting on a log.
The first jumped off when it heard the dog.
> Froggy, froggy, froggy loggy dog

Four little froggies sitting on a log.
The second one left for its morning jog.
> Froggy, froggy, froggy loggy jog

Three little froggies sitting on a log.
The third one vanished in the morning fog.
> Froggy, froggy, froggy loggy fog

Two little froggies sitting on a log.
The fourth one slipped as it played leap frog.
> Froggy, froggy, froggy loggy frog

One little froggy sitting on a log.
All alone, it is the top dog frog.
> Froggy, froggy,
> top dog frog

Monday

Using the patterns on page 53, make five frogs and a log to use in introducing this poem.

Recite the poem, removing a frog from the log after each verse.

Explain the meaning of the expression "top dog." Ask students to tell why the one frog is now the "top dog frog."

Repeat the poem, encouraging students to join in on the refrain.

Tuesday

Review the poem:
- Recite the first verse and have students identify the two rhyming words. (log, dog)
- Practice stretching the two words into phonemes. (/l/ /o/ /g/ and /d/ /o/ /g/)
- Do the same for each of the -og family words.

Five little froggies sitting on a log.
The first jumped off when it heard the dog.
Froggy, froggy, froggy loggy dog

Four little froggies sitting on a log.
The second one left for its morning jog.
Froggy, froggy, froggy loggy jog

Three little froggies sitting on a log.
The third one vanished in the morning fog.
Froggy, froggy, froggy loggy fog

Two little froggies sitting on a log.
The fourth one slipped as it played leap frog.
Froggy, froggy, froggy loggy frog

One little froggy sitting on a log.
All alone, it is the top dog frog.
Froggy, froggy,
top dog frog

Wednesday

Recite the poem together.

Act out the poem with five students acting as frogs. "Frogs" hop to their places as students recite the refrain.

Thursday

Recite poem and act it out until all students have had a chance to be a frog.

Friday

Write the poem words in the **-og** family on the chalkboard.
  (log, dog, jog, fog, frog)
Have students repeat the words stretching them into individual phonemes.
  log - /l/ /o/ /g/
After each word, repeat the refrain ending with the word stretched.
  (Froggy, froggy, froggy-loggy, [log])
End with a final recitation of the poem.

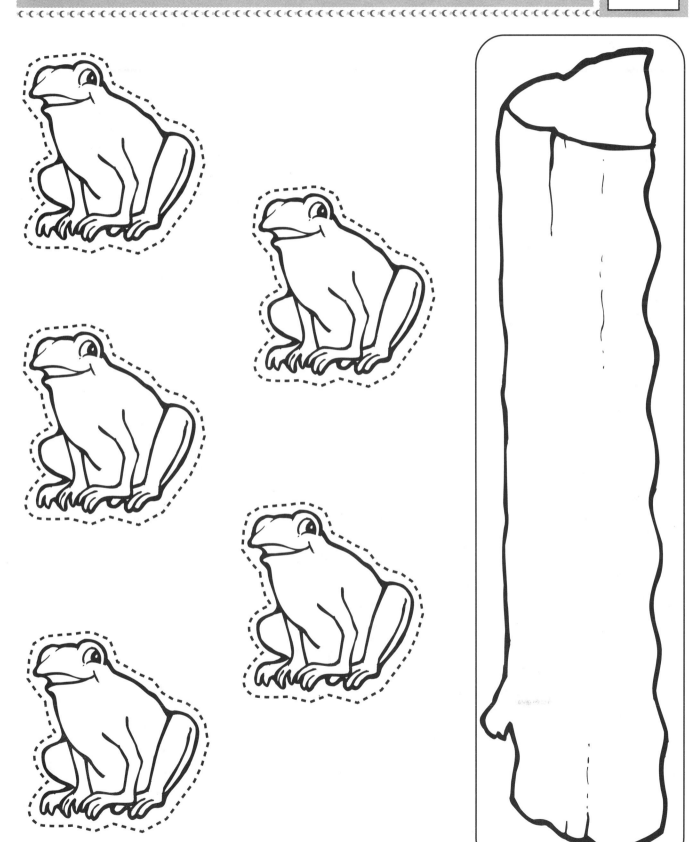

Listen for words that begin with the same sound as you look at the colors all around.

Colors all around

Pink, pink, pink pigs

Yellow, yellow, yellow yarn

Blue, blue, blue blossoms

Green, green, green grass

Red, red, red radishes

Black, black, black beans

Colors all around.

 Phonemic Awareness • EMC 740

Monday

Ask students to think about the colors all around them as you read the color chant.

Ask students to recall the six objects named in the chant. Take a few minutes to talk about whether the students have ever seen the things described.

Read the chant again.

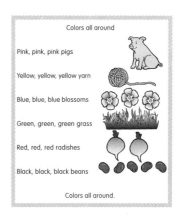

Colors all around

Pink, pink, pink pigs

Yellow, yellow, yellow yarn

Blue, blue, blue blossoms

Green, green, green grass

Red, red, red radishes

Black, black, black beans

Colors all around.

Tuesday

Review the color chant:
- Teacher says the color words in each line; students name the object.
- After reviewing the phrases, identify the pattern in each.
  (The color is repeated three times and then an object of the color is named. The object must start with the same sound as the color.)
- Read the phrases again.

Wednesday

Review the color chant:
- Teacher recites the first line, "Colors all around," and then holds up a piece of pink paper. Students recall and say, "Pink, pink, pink pigs."
- Repeat with the remaining five colors.

Ask students to identify things around them that are the colors described.
   (Pink—Sally's shirt, Tamara's headband, Dan's pencil, etc.)
Then ask if any of the things named would fit the pattern in the phrases.
   (Dan's pencil would fit since pencil begins with the same sound as pink.)

Write the new phrases on a chart.
   (Pink, pink, pink pencil)

Thursday

Review the chant as a group.
Have students choose a new color and make a phrase that fits that color.
   (Brown, brown, brown branch)
Repeat with several colors.

Friday

Create a class book, *Colors All Around*:
- Reproduce the book page form on page 56.
- Have each student choose a color and draw a thing that is that color and begins with the same sound as the color name.
- An adult writes each child's patterned phrase on his/her book page, for example:
       Purple, purple, purple petunias
- Staple the individual pages together and read the book.

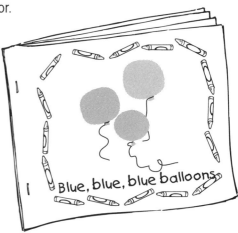

Blue, blue, blue balloons

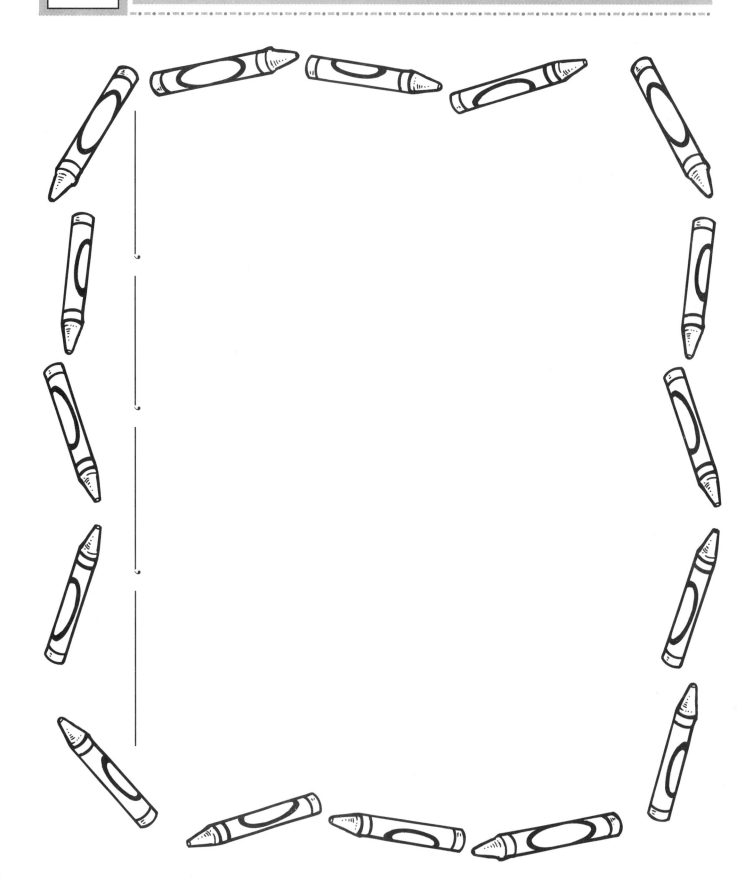

Phonemic Awareness • EMC 740

Listen to the sounds around you and then match them in this silly verse.

Do you hear the bell?
Can you hear it ding?
    Dingy, ding, ding, ding
    Dingy, ding, ding, ding

Do you hear the clock?
Can you hear it tick?
    Ticky, tick, tick, tick
    Ticky, tick, tick, tick

Do you hear the trumpet?
Can you hear it toot?
    Tooty, toot, toot, toot
    Tooty, toot, toot, toot

Do you hear the baby?
Can you hear it coo?
    Cooey coo, coo, coo
    Cooey coo, coo, coo

Monday

Talk about the sounds that you hear every day. Then read the verse.

Read the verse again, with students joining in on the sound refrains.

Tuesday

Recite the poem in three different ways:
- students whisper the sound refrains.
- students loudly speak the sound refrains.
- students clap the sound refrains.

Wednesday

Review the poem. Students may be ready to say the entire verse with you. Holding up pictures of a bell, a clock, a trumpet, and a baby will help to cue them for the next part of the verse.

Focus on the sound words. Have students identify the position of sounds on the words. For example:

ding
- Do you hear /d/ at the beginning, in the middle, or at the end?
  tick
- Where do you hear /k/?

Do you hear the bell?
Can you hear it ding?
   Dingy, ding, ding, ding
   Dingy, ding, ding, ding

Do you hear the clock?
Can you hear it tick?
   Ticky, tick, tick, tick
   Ticky, tick, tick, tick

Do you hear the trumpet?
Can you hear it toot?
   Tooty, toot, toot, toot
   Tooty, toot, toot, toot

Do you hear the baby?
Can you hear it coo?
   Cooey coo, coo, coo
   Cooey coo, coo, coo

Thursday

Have students choose an object in the classroom that makes a sound. Use the sound to create a new verse for the poem.

Do you hear the door?
Can you hear it creak?
Creaky, creak, creak, creak
Creaky, creak, creak, creak

Friday

Have students individually choose an object that makes a sound that they have heard. Have them illustrate the sound on the form on page 59. An adult can write the name of the thing making the sound and the sound. Students "read" their pages. The class provides the sound refrains.

Do you hear the **dog**?
Can you hear it **bark**?

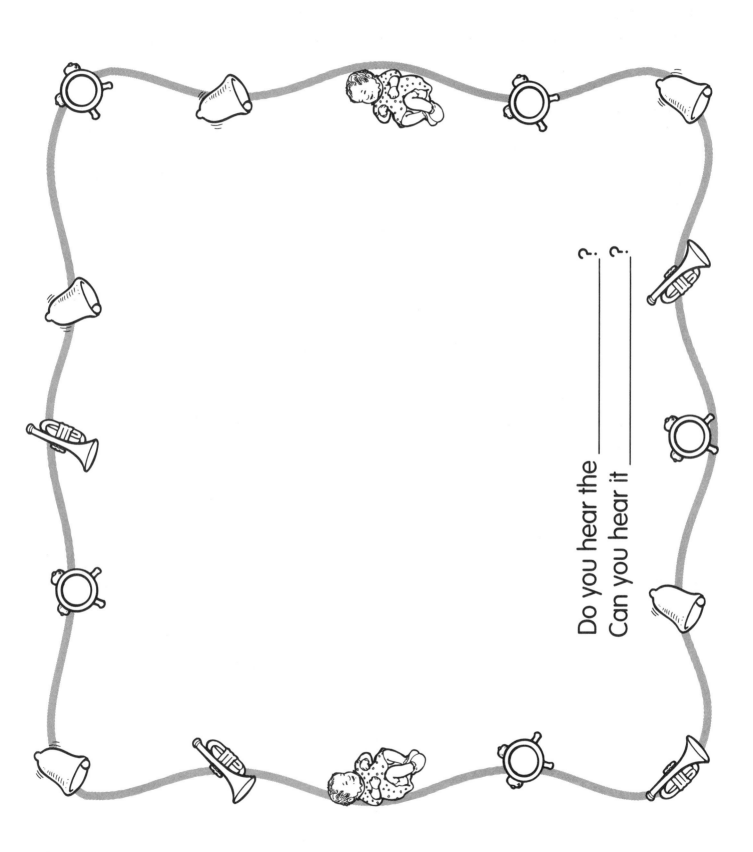

Do you hear the _____?
Can you hear it _____?

Sing this song to the tune of "If You're Happy and You Know It."

If your name begins with _____,
stand up now.

If your name begins with _____,
stand up now.

If your name begins with _____,
stand up and take a bow.

If your name begins with _____,
stand up now.

Monday

Fill in the each blank with the same phoneme (sound) as you sing this song to the tune of "If You're Happy and You Know It."

Students should stand if their name begins with the phoneme. Ask students to "sound off" saying their names aloud when the verse is over.

Substitute different phonemes and repeat.

Tuesday

Sing the song again, using more phonemes until each student has had a turn to stand.

Wednesday

Choose a student leader to choose the phoneme and lead the class in singing. Repeat several times.

Thursday

Choose several different movements and change the song. For example:

If your name begins with _____, wiggle now.
If your name begins with _____, sit down now.
If your name begins with _____, signal now.
If your name begins with _____, salute now.

Friday

Create a graph as you sing the song today.

Tell students that you will move to a new spot (along a baseline) each time the song is sung. When they hear the sound the begins their first name, they are to line up one behind another in front of you.

If your name begins with _____, stand right here.
If your name begins with _____, stand right here.
If your name begins with _____, stand here and give a cheer. Yeah!
If your name begins with _____, stand right here.

When all children are standing, count to see which line is longest.

If it is appropriate for your students, create a picture graph to represent this real graph. Reproduce the patterns on page 62. Each student writes his/her name on a square and places it on a chart under the corresponding beginning letter.

This chant allows students to practice sound matching and also to match sounds to letters.

I'm going to the store.

I think I'll buy some more...

Monday

Recite the couplet. Tell students that everything that you put in your shopping bag must begin with an /m/. Have students "shop" around the room for items that would fit in the bag.

Substitute other target sounds.

I'm going to the store.
I think I'll buy some more...

Tuesday

Recite the couplet. Write a target sound on a shopping bag. Have students "shop" around the room for items that would fit in the sound bag.

Wednesday

Set out a variety of objects or pictures. Label several baskets with the different letter cards. Have students recite the couplet and choose an object, placing the object in the appropriate basket.

Thursday

Use real lunch bags or give each student an empty sack pattern. (Reproduce the patterns on page 65.)

Ask them to put an object in the bag or to draw an object on the sack pattern that begins with a target sound.

Friday

Let the students designate a target sound for their individual sacks. Then have them locate or draw three things that have that target sound.

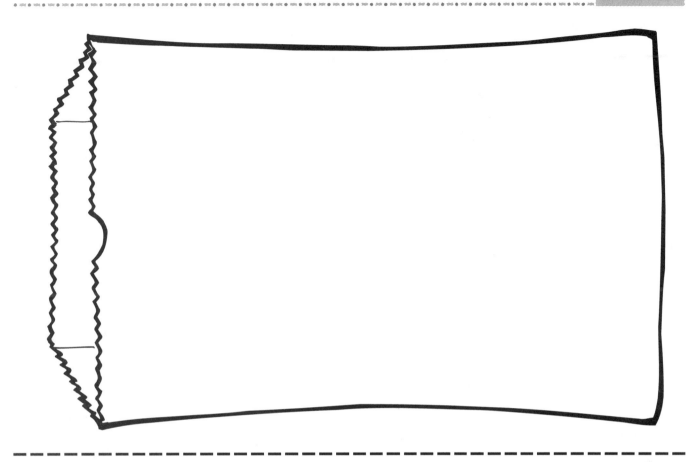

Isolate phonemes in this chant as you stir up a perfect purple pie.

Making a purple pie — yum, yum

Making a purple pie

With purple berries

And purple cherries

And _____

All in a purple pie.

Hi there, _____.

Glad you stopped by.

Nice to see you here

in my purple pie.

Monday

Recite the poem for the students:
- Use a big tub or a box as your "bowl."
- Stir with a pretend spoon.
- When you come to the blank say one of your students' names. That student jumps in the bowl to become part of the purple pie.

Repeat, using a different student's name.

Making a purple pie — yum, yum
Making a purple pie
  With purple berries
  And purple cherries
  And _____
All in a purple pie.

Hi there, _____
Glad you stopped by.
Nice to see you here
in my purple pie.

Tuesday

Recite the poem, using different students' names until all have had a turn.

Wednesday

Help students to stretch their names into individual phonemes.
For example:

> Tony = /t/ /o/ /n/ /e/
> Susan = /s/ /oo/ /z/ /u/ /n/

Explain that the next time you play the purple pie game you will name the students in the pie by stretching their names.

Thursday

Play the purple pie game. Name students by stretching their names.

> ...And /t/ /o/ /m/
> all in a purple pie.

The student jumps in the bowl and the class blends the name responding:

> Hi there, Tom
> Glad you stopped by...

Friday

Reproduce the pattern on page 68. After playing the purple pie game, have each student draw themselves in the purple pie picture.

A Perfect Purple Pie

My Name

A Perfect Purple Pie

Make fur or felt kittens to pet with this lesson on phoneme segmentation and syllable splitting

Kitty

Pretty kitty

Itty-bitty kitty

Pretty itty-bitty kitty

Meow

Kitty
Pretty kitty
Itty-bitty kitty
Pretty itty-bitty kitty
Meow

Monday

Introduce the poem with a stuffed kitten:
- Recite the poem and stroke the kitten to the syllable beat.
- Let students echo as many lines at a time as are appropriate.

Tuesday

Have students make a kitten using the pattern on page 71.
Students recite poem with you, stroking the kitten to the syllable beat.

Wednesday

Half of the students stroke and recite while the other half count the beats. (Students should determine that each line adds two beats until the final line.)

Thursday

Ask students to stretch the word kitty into phonemes.
(/k/ /i/ /t/ /e/)
Recite the poem adding the phonemes for kitty after the first four lines.

    Kitty /k/ /i/ /t/ /e/
    Pretty kitty /k/ /i/ /t/ /e/
    Itty-bitty kitty /k/ /i/ /t/ /e/
    Pretty itty-bitty kitty /k/ /i/ /t/ /e/
    Meow

Friday

Have students use their own words to describe kittens.
Create poems using their words.

    Kitty
    Funny kitty
    Playful, funny kitty
    Meow

Stretch "sticky" words apart (phoneme segmentation) and let them squish back together (phoneme blending).

ooey gooey

ishy squishy

icky sticky

Wash your hands!!

ooey gooey
ishy squishy
icky sticky
Wash your hands!!

Monday

Recite the verse. Ask students to describe things that might be gooey or squishy or sticky. Record their responses.

Choose one child to act as the "mother" or "teacher" and to say the line "Wash your hands!!" as the rest of the class recites the words, rubs their hands together, and makes faces to represent "the mess."

Tuesday

Reproduce the picture cards on page 74.

Recite the verse. Show the bubble gum, glue, and cotton candy picture cards. (You may want to make other cards for the responses given by your students on Monday if they are not pictured).

Ask students to stretch sticky words into phonemes as they pretend to stretch it apart with their fingers.
　　　　(/g/ /l/ /oo/)
Then clap hands together and say the word.
　　　　(glue)

Wednesday

Spray a tiny bit of shaving cream on students' hands. Ask them to describe how it feels. (squishy)

Continue with Tuesday's activity using mud, sponge, and shaving cream picture cards.

Thursday

Have students tell something that they did to get gooey.
　　I fell in a mud puddle.　　　　I frosted my cupcakes.
Class stretches the gooey word into phonemes.
　　/m/ /u/ /d/　　　　　　/f/ /r/ /o/ /s/ /t/ /i/ /ng/
Then recite the verse, adding the new word at the end.
　　ooey gooey　　ishy squishy　　icky sticky MUD
　　ooey gooey　　ishy squishy　　icky sticky FROSTING

Friday

Have students repeat yesterday's activity telling about another messy experience. For example:

Getting jam on your hands.
/j/ /a/ /m/

　　ooey gooey　　ishy squishy　　icky sticky JAM

Practice phoneme segmentation, blending, and matching letters to sounds as you create a Piggy Bank Directory for the members of your class. (Repeat to the rhythm of "Who Stole the Cookies?")

Who stole the pennies from the piggy bank?

_____ stole the pennies from the piggy bank.

Who me?
　　　Yes, you.
Couldn't be.
　　　Then who?

_____ stole the pennies from the piggy bank.

Oh, _____ stole the pennies from the piggy bank.

Monday

Teach and play the game:
- Class sits in a circle on the floor.
- Everyone claps and slaps legs to establish rhythm. (This continues throughout the game.)
- Together all repeat — Who stole the pennies from the piggy bank?
- Leader starts by naming a student — **Dougie** stole the pennies from the piggy bank.
- Student replies — Who me?
- Class says — Yes, you.
- Student says — Couldn't be.
- Class asks — Then who?
- Student answers — **Mary** stole the pennies from the piggy bank.
- Class responds — Oh, **Mary** stole the pennies from the piggy bank.
- New student replies —Who me?... and the game continues

Who stole the pennies from the piggy bank?
_____ stole the pennies from the piggy bank.

Who me?
Yes you.
Couldn't be.
Then who?

_____ stole the pennies from the piggy bank.
Oh, _____ stole the pennies from the piggy bank.

Tuesday

Review the game. Enjoy the rhythm!

Wednesday

Teacher preparation:
- Reproduce the piggy bank pattern on page 77— one for each letter of the alphabet, perhaps more than one if you have a large number of students whose first names begin with a particular letter.
- Write one letter of the alphabet on each piggy bank.
- Glue student photos on the appropriate pages. (All students whose names begin with A have pictures pasted on the A bank.)

After playing the game today, show several of the piggy bank letter pages.
- Point to students' pictures and say the names slowly.
- Have students identify the phonemes as you write corresponding letters under the photos on the letter page.
- Then have students blend the letter sounds together to read the name of the student.

Thursday

Play the game. Continue to work on the piggy bank directory.

Friday

Play the game. Finish and post the piggy bank directory.

You'll love the way the words feel as you say them. Notice the changes as you substitute phonemes.

Bibbity, bobbity, boo
What shall we do?

Bibbity, bobbity, bee
Come and play with me.

Bibbity, bobbity, bay
Let's have fun today.

Monday

Teach the couplets by having the class echo one line at a time.

Tuesday

Review the rhyme.
Ask students to echo each couplet.

Have students identify rhyming words.

Bibbity, bobbity, boo
What shall we do?

Bibbity, bobbity, bee
Come and play with me.

Bibbity, bobbity, bay
Let's have fun today.

Wednesday

Repeat the couplets as you play this game:
- Form two equal lines. Students stand behind each other. The first student in each line faces the other across a space of about ten feet.
- The first student in each line walks across the space between the lines as the class chants, "Bibbity, bobbity, boo."
- The two students meet and shake hands saying, "What shall we do?"
- The class chants, "Bibbity, bobbity, bee."
- The two students move off together saying, "Come and play with me." They sit down in a predesignated area.
- Continue the game with the next students in line. After the last pair says, "Come and play with me," the entire class chants the last couplet.

Thursday

Talk about the pattern of the couplets. (The ending words rhyme. The first line says Bibbity, bobbity, and the last word begins with b. The second line has 4 or 5 beats.)
Have students tell what the first line would be if the second lines were:
    How do you feel? (Bibbity, bobbity, beel)
    I'm feeling fine. (Bibbity, bobbity, bine)
    Let's go to lunch. (Bibbity, boobity, bunch)

Friday

Compose a new couplet:
    Hint: Start with the second line naming an activity.
    Then rhyme the first line with it.
        (Bibbity, bobbity, bide.
        Let's go outside.)

Reproduce page 80. Have students draw a self-portrait and make new couplets using their names.
An adult can circulate and do the writing while the students draw. For example:

    Bibbity, bobbity, bott   My name is Scott.

Bibbity, bobbity, b_organ_
My name is _Morgan_ .

Bibbity, bobbity, b

My name is _____ .

In this week's activities, students listen to alliteration and substitute onsets to make new couplets.

Wiggle waggle wog
Watch the dog.

Wiggle waggle wug
Watch the bug.

Wiggle waggle waterpillar
Watch the caterpillar.

Wiggle waggle weetle
Watch the beetle.

Monday

Introduce the couplets:
- Say all four couplets through one time.
- Then repeat one couplet at a time, having students listen for words that begin with the same sound. (Each couplet has four words that begin with the w sound.)
- Talk about the words the students heard.

Wiggle waggle wog
Watch the dog.

Wiggle waggle wug
Watch the bug.

Wiggle waggle waterpillar
Watch the caterpillar.

Wiggle waggle weetle
Watch the beetle.

Tuesday

Act out the couplets as you repeat them:
- Choose students to imitate each animal.
- When the couplet about the animal is read, those students perform the actions of the animal.

Wednesday

Say the couplets together. Have students describe the pattern of each couplet.
(The first line says *Wiggle, waggle, w_____*.
The second line says *Watch the* [name of an animal].
The last word in the first line rhymes with the name of the animal.)

Together compose a new couplet:
- Ask a student to suggest the name of a new animal.
  Talk about what would happen to the word if it were to start with /w/.
- Say the new couplet together, for example:
    Wiggle, waggle, wiger
    Watch the tiger.

Thursday

Reproduce the form on page 83 so that students can compose a couplet of their own. As students draw the picture of their animal, an adult can circulate and write each student's couplet as he/she tells the name of the animal and the /w/ word that rhymes with the animal's name.

Friday

Celebrate a week of wiggle-waggling by having students read their original couplets.
Bind the couplets into a Wiggle Waggle Book.

Wiggle, waggle, w**ig**_____
Watch the ____**pig**_____

Wiggle, waggle, w _____.

Watch the _____.

Develop vocabulary as you substitute phonemes in this question/answer chant.

Fee-Fi-Fo-Fum
Where is your thumb?

Fee-Fi-Fo-Fum
This is my thumb.

Fee-Fi-Fo-Fear
Where is your ear?

Fee-Fi-Fo-Fear
This is my ear.

Fee-Fi-Fum-Fee
Where is your knee?

Fee-Fi-Fo-Fee
This is my knee.

Monday

Say the poem one time for the class.
Then play the question/answer game:
- You ask the question: Fee-Fi-Fo-Fum   Where is your thumb?
- Students give the answers: Fee-Fi-Fo-Fum   This is my thumb.

Continue for all six verses.
Ask students to identify the rhyming words in each question.

Fee-Fi-Fo-Fum
Where is your thumb?

Fee-Fi-Fo-Fum
This is my thumb.

Fee-Fi-Fo-Fear
Where is your ear?

Fee-Fi-Fo-Fear
This is my ear.

Fee-Fi-Fum-Fee
Where is your knee?

Fee-Fi-Fo-Fee
This is my knee.

Tuesday

Play the question/answer game again with new questions:

Fee-Fi-Fo Fummy
Where is your tummy?

Fee-Fi-Fo Fed
Where is your head?

Fee-Fi-Fo-Fair
Where is your hair?

Help students to identify the onsets and rimes of the rhyming words:
f — ummy   t — ummy   f — ed   h — ead   f — air   h — air

Wednesday

Add more new questions:
Fee-Fi-Fo-Farm.
Where is your arm?

Fee-Fi-Fo-Felbow.
Where is your elbow?

Fee-Fi-Fo-Fin
Where is your chin?

As a class make up a new question. For example:

Fee-Fi-Fo-Foo
Where is your shoe?

Thursday

Play the question/answer game, letting the students ask the questions.

Friday

Reproduce the form on page 86. Have each student create a Fee-Fi-Fo question and illustrate it. Make a class book and read it together.

Fee-Fi-Fo-F unch
Where is your lunch ?

Reproduce this page for individual students for Friday's activity.

Fee-Fi-Fo-F

Where is your _____ ?

"I Spy" is a fun way to practice phonemic substitution, blending and sound/letter matching.

See the ball.
Is that all?

See the bear
Over there.

See the snake.
Take a break.

See the tree.
Can it be?

See the sock.
What a shock!

Monday

Have students make paper spyglasses using the pattern on page 89. (They will use them each day this week.)

See the ball.
Is that all?

See the bear
Over there.

See the snake.
Take a break.

See the tree.
Can it be?

See the sock.
What a shock!

Play an I Spy game:
- Display a ball.
- Say, "See the ball."
- Students look through their spyglasses at the ball.
- They stretch the word into individual phonemes. /b/ /a/ /l/
- Then blend the sounds together and say, "ball."
- You say, "Is that all?"
- Have students peer around for other objects that rhyme with ball.
- Prompt students, "See the wall," or have students point out rhyming objects.
  (wall   hall   doll   Paul   shawl)
- Stretch and blend the new words.

Tuesday

Use the spyglasses and repeat the Monday's activity with the second couplet. (Use a teddy bear)

See the bear.
Over there.   (chair   hair   pear   square   stair   air)

Wednesday

Use the spyglasses and repeat the activity with the third couplet. (Use a rubber snake or a picture of a snake.)

See the snake.
Take a break. (cake lake rake   stake   Jake   snowflake)

Thursday

Use the spyglasses and repeat the activity with the next couplet. (Use a picture of a tree, or point out the window if there's a tree outside.)

See the tree.
Can it be?   (bee knee key pea   three   monkey   sea)

Friday

Use the spyglasses and repeat the activity with the final couplet. (Make a really large sock from fabric with a wild design so that it fits the verse.)

See the sock.
What a shock! (block chalk   clock   lock   rock   smock)

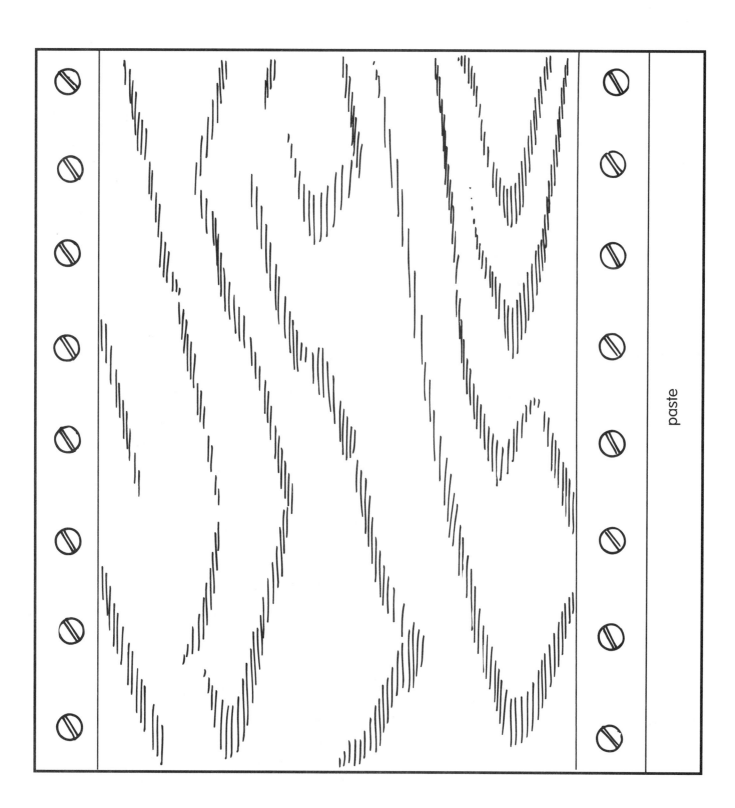

paste

Sing this song to the tune of "London Bridge" as you practice phoneme isolation and sound/letter matching.

Tell me, tell me,
   what you hear...
   what you hear...
   what you hear.

What's the first sound
in your ear?
My fair _____.

Monday

Sing and play the game:
- Have students sit in a circle.
- Everyone sings as the leader walks around the circle behind the students.
- At the blank the leader taps the shoulder of the nearest student and sings the student's name. (Add /o/ or /e/-/o/ to the end of names in order to make them three syllables, for example,
    My fair Susan-o
    My fair Dave-e-o
- The class names the phoneme that begins that student's name.
- The student becomes the new leader.

Tell me, tell me,
what you hear...
what you hear...
what you hear.

What's the first sound in your ear?
My fair _____.

Tuesday

Sing and play the game again until all students have been chosen at least once.

Wednesday

Display alphabet cards (pages 105-111) in the front of the room. As you play the game today, have a student point to the letter that stands for the phoneme you hear at the beginning of the name. (Make a fun "ear" pointer using the pattern on page 92.)

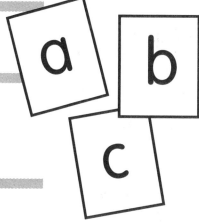

Thursday

Sing and play the game with the leader walking around the room and choosing an object instead of a student. Let the students use the ear pointer to tap the objects.

Friday

Try playing the game outside on the playground. When you come back inside, list the things that you found on the playground.

Choose the letters from the alphabet cards that stand for the phonemes that you hear at the beginning of each thing.

Reproduce this pattern and fasten to the end of a ruler, straw, or dowel to make a pointer for use with the games on Wednesday and Thursday.

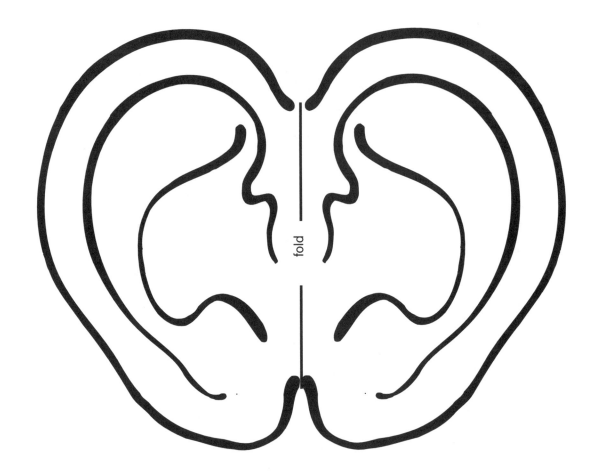

fold

Practice describing and substituting phonemes to create a new verse every day.

See the cat.

Big black cat.

How 'bout that!

Monday

Recite the verse. Talk about different kinds of cats.
Create "copy cat" poems about different cats.
Notice that each line has three beats.

See the cat.	See the cat.
Purring cat.	Small gray cat.
How 'bout that!	How 'bout that!

See the cat.
Big black cat.
How 'bout that!

Tuesday

Place the letters for cat, one by one, in a pocket chart.
Have students say each phoneme separately as you place
letters in the chart, then blend the sounds together to form the word.

Replace the **c** with an **h** and have students say
the phonemes and then blend the sounds to
make the new word, *hat*.

Repeat the poem activity creating a describing poem
for a hat. Remind students that each line of the poem
must have only three beats.

See the hat.
Red ball hat.
How 'bout that!

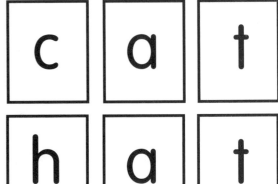

Wednesday

Place the letters for cat, one by one, in a pocket chart.
Have students say the individual phonemes and then
blend them into the word **cat**. Substitute the **h**. Students
read **hat**; then substitute an **r** for the **h** and blend the new
word, **rat**.

Repeat the poem activity creating a describing poem for a rat.
See the rat.
Skinny rat.
How 'bout that!

Thursday

Using letter cards in a pocket chart, move from
cat to **hat** to **rat** to **bat**.
Repeat the poem activity, creating a describing poem for a bat.
(Try doing a poem for a both a flying bat and a baseball bat.)

Friday

Use letter cards to make today's new word—**mat**.
Reproduce the pattern on page 95 for students to decorate
and create their own mat poem.

See the mat.
The **spotted** mat.
How 'bout that!

Phonemic Awareness • EMC 740

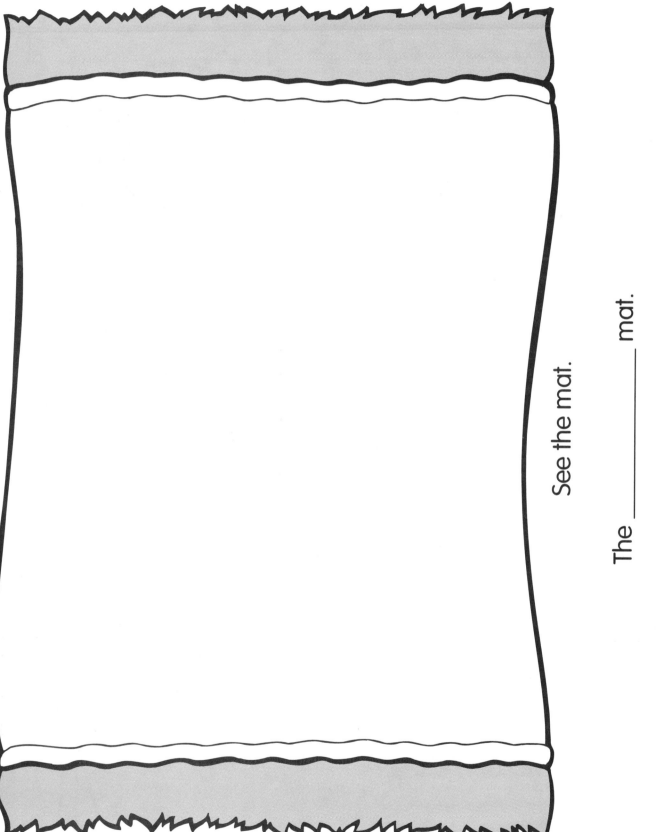

See the mat.

The _____ mat.

How 'bout that!

Use water drops to create drippy words, blending and deleting phonemes, and matching sounds to letters.

Drip, drop, drip, drop rain
The water goes down the drain.

Drip, drop, drip, drop sink
I think I'll take a drink.

Drip, drop, drip, drop shower
This might take an hour.

Phonemic Awareness • EMC 740

Monday

Recite the poem to the class. Have students echo one or two lines at a time. Then place letters for the word drip, one by one, into a pocket chart.

Have students say each phoneme separately as you place the letters in the chart, then blend the sounds together to form the word. Substitute the **o** card for the **i** card to create drop.

Tuesday

Begin with a quick review of drip and drop with the letter cards. Change the **i** and the **o** cards quickly as students read **drip**, **drop**, **drip**, **drop**.

Recite the poem.
Have students determine what the words rain, sink, and shower have in common. (They all have water. They all have drips.)

Wednesday

Recite the poem. Ask students to take away the first sound in each word in the drip line.
   drip becomes rip   drop becomes rop
Use the letter cards to show deleting the sounds.

Thursday

Reproduce the droplet patterns on page 98. After reciting the poem, have students identify the individual phonemes in drop. (/d/ /r/ /o/ /p/)

Teacher writes the letters that represent the phonemes on droplets.
        d   r   o   p
Have students arrange the droplets so that they form the word and read it.

Friday

Have students think of other drippy things and places. Create droplet words using their ideas.
Then read them. For example:
    Drip, drop, drip, drop (faucet/downspout)

Drip, drop, drip, drop rain
The water goes down the drain.

Drip, drop, drip, drop sink
I think I'll take a drink.

Drip, drop, drip, drop shower
This might take an hour.

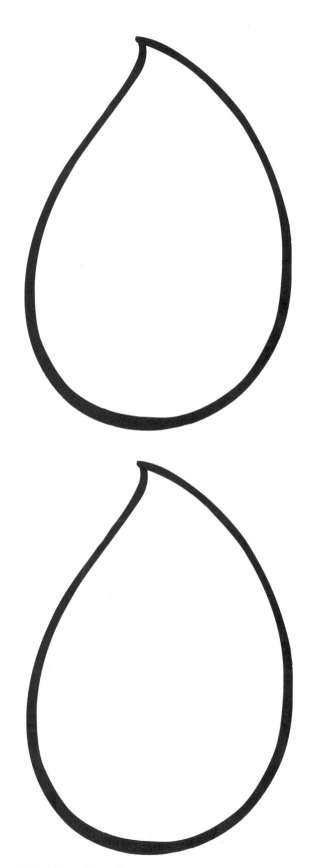
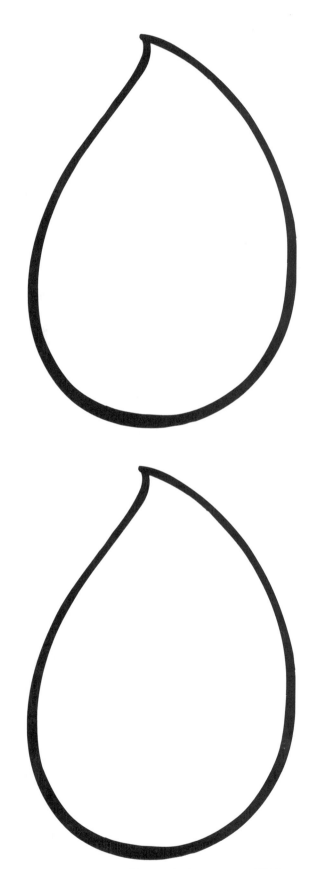

Focus on a different fruit or vegetable each day as you substitute and blend phonemes and match sounds to letters.

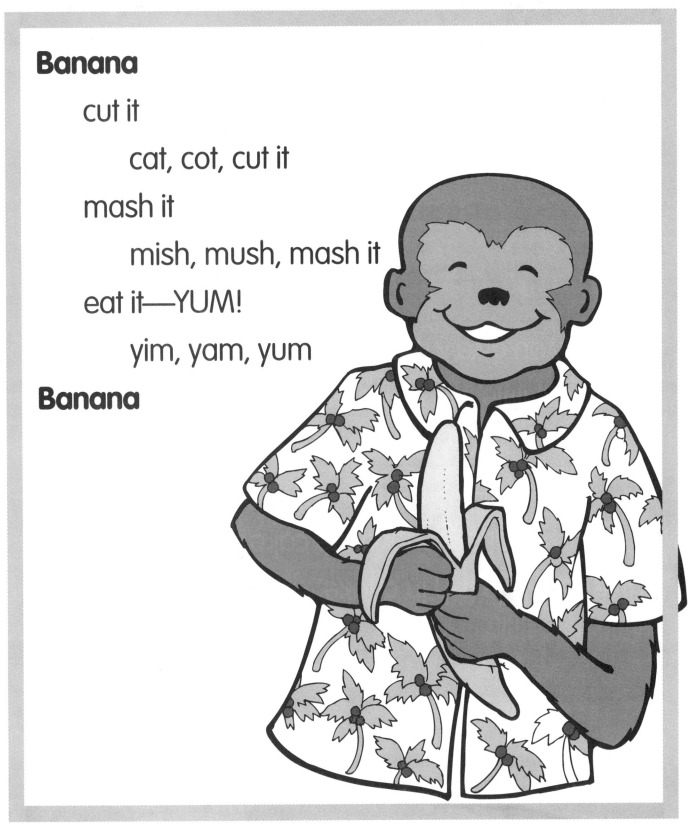

Banana

cut it

cat, cot, cut it

mash it

mish, mush, mash it

eat it—YUM!

yim, yam, yum

Banana

Monday

Bring a banana to class to display as you recite the verse.
Use the alphabet cards (pages 105-111) to spell **cut**.
Remove the **u** and have students substitute different
vowel cards to make **cat** and **cot**.
Repeat with **mash** and **yum**.

Banana
  cut it
    cat cot cut it
  mash it
    mish mush mash it
  eat it YUM!
    yim yam yum
Banana

Tuesday

Bring an apple to class. Talk about what
you do to an apple.

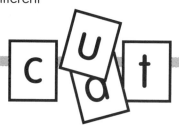

Choose two action words and rewrite the verse,
leaving the eat it phrase intact.

Apple
    bake it   bike, boke, bake it
    slice it   sluce, sleece, slice it
    eat it YUM   yim, yam, yum
Apple

Record your new verse on the form on page 101.

Wednesday

Repeat the activities with a lemon, or another fruit or vegetable
appropriate for your class. Try to elicit new verbs, for example,
squeeze, peel, seed.

Record the verse on the form on page 92.

Thursday

Repeat the activities with a carrot. Verb choices might
include chop, dice, slice.

Record the verse.

Friday

Repeat the activities with a potato. Try the verbs mash, fry, boil.

Record the verse. Put all the pages together for a class book.

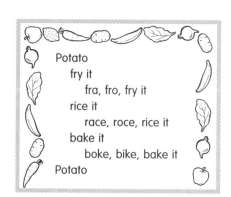

Potato
  fry it
    fra, fro, fry it
  rice it
    race, roce, rice it
  bake it
    boke, bike, bake it
Potato

Phonemic Awareness • EMC 740

These couplets provide practice with word families and involve phoneme substitution, blending, and matching sounds to letters.

Little fish, Little fish in the dish,
Can you help me with my wish?

Little fish, little fish in a lake,
Can you make a chocolate cake?

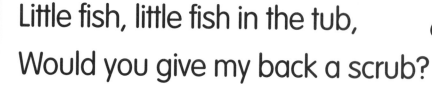

Little fish, little fish in the tub,
Would you give my back a scrub?

Monday

Introduce the couplets:
- Say the rhyme to the students.
- Let students echo one or two lines at a time.
- Have students identify the rhyming words in each couplet.
  (fish, dish, wish)   (lake, cake)   (tub, scrub)

Little fish, Little fish in the dish,
Can you help me with my wish?

Little fish, little fish in a lake,
Can you make a chocolate cake?

Little fish, little fish in the tub,
Would you give my back a scrub?

Tuesday

Recite the couplets together. Tell students that they will create
words by listening to word families and adding beginning sounds:
- Start with the **-ish** family.
- Say the word-family sound **-ish**. Use the alphabet cards
  (pages 105-111) to spell **ish** in the pocket chart.
- Students make words that belong to the **-ish** family. Students say
  the word and then identify the letter(s) to complete the word.
  (wish — w   dish — d   fish — f   swish — sw)
- Record the words on an **-ish** family list.

Wednesday

Recite the couplets. Have students read the **-ish** family list:
- One student points to each letter with the fish pointer
  (page 104) as the others say each phoneme separately.
- Then move the pointer quickly across the letters as the
  students blend the sounds together to form the word.
Create an **-ake** family list in the same manner as was done for **-ish**.

Thursday

Recite the couplets. Review the **-ish** word list and the **-ake** list in
the same way as done on Wednesday.

Create an **-ub** family list.

Friday

Recite the couplets. Read the **-ish**, **-ake**, and **-ub** family lists.

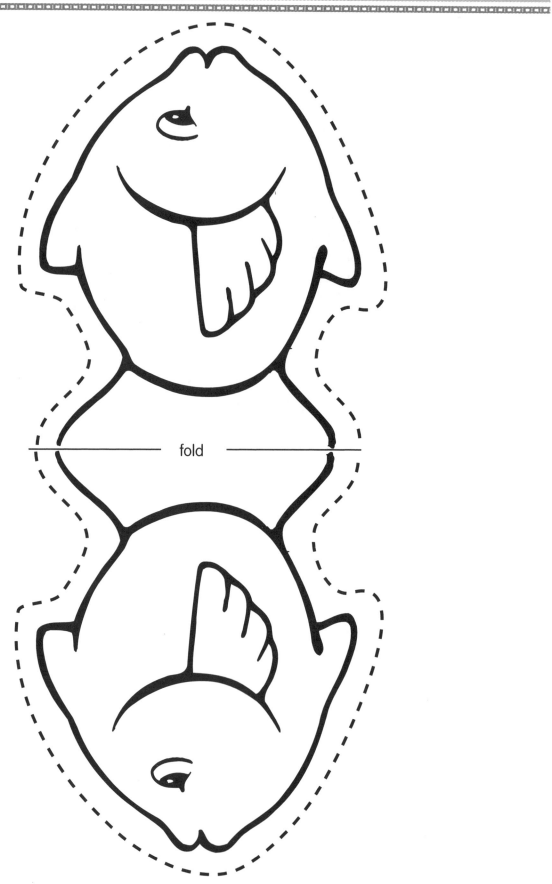

fold

Alphabet Cards

a

b

c

d

e f

g h

i j

k l

m n

o p

q r

s t

u v

w x

y z

yes no

Student Inventory

Reproduce this inventory for each student. Give it orally to individuals, stopping at the point where the student misses two in a row. Record student responses on the page.

Name_____   Date _____

Level 1 Rhythm and Rhyme

Whole Word Discrimination
Ask, "Are these words the same?" Record response: **y** for yes and **n** for no.

cat - cat _____   pan - pat _____   big - bug _____

fly - fly _____   day - way _____   tree - tree _____

Rhyming Words — Recognition
Ask, "Do these words rhyme?" Record response: **y** for yes and **n** for no.

run - sun _____   play - ball _____   hook - book _____

Rhyming Words — Application
Ask, "What word rhymes with _____?" Record the response.

bat _____   eat _____   skip _____

Syllable Counting
Ask, "How many syllables (word parts) do you hear?" Record the response.

lion _____   horse _____   elephant _____ tyrannosaurus _____

Level 2 Parts of a Word

Syllable Segmentation
Say, "I'll say a word, you repeat it slowly."
Demonstrate: cowboy = cow-boy
Mark ⊕ if student is successful, mark ⊖ if not.

sandwich _____   hammer _____   grasshopper _____

Oral Synthesis — Blending Speech Sounds
Say, "Listen and tell the word. /p/ /u/ /p/ — pup." Record the response.

/g/ /o/ _____   /t/ /e/ /n/ /t/ _____   /c/ /a/ /t/ _____